Alexander Korotko

Irrazionalismo

Translated from the Russian
by Anatoly Kudryavitsky

SurVision Books

First published in 2019 by
SurVision Books
Dublin, Ireland
www.survisionmagazine.com

Copyright © Alexander Korotko, 2019

Translations © Anatoly Kudryavitsky, 2018, 2019

Cover image © Vince McGreal, 2019

Design © SurVision Books, 2019

ISBN: 978-1-912963-06-5

This book is in copyright. No part of this publication may be reproduced, stored in a retrieval system, or transmitted in any form or by any means without the prior permission in writing from the publisher.

Acknowledgements

Snow, Desert, and *The Past* originally appeared in *SurVision Magazine.*

CONTENTS

Wars	4
The Flood	6
Time	7
A Water-Melon Plantation	8
Trembita	9
Troy	10
Rendezvous	11
The Plot	12
Happiness	13
The Sea	14
The Air	15
Souls	16
Night	17
The World	18
Falling Stars	19
The Sense of Time	20
Parallel Lines	21
September	22
Hope	23
Dreams	24
Autumn	25
Snow	26
Desert	27
The Past	28
Spring Air	29
Soundlessness	30
Unspoken Words	31
Words	32
Chill	33
Silence	34
Word	35
Rain	36
Love	37
Life	38
A Disparate Life	39
After the Storm	40

Wars

The icebergs of souls
under a blue
sail
on an ice-floe cloud,
on a feather bed,
floating through the looking glass
of inconsolable
dreams.
There are no stars left
on the uniforms
of the careless.
Armoured trains
rest
at the eternal
stations,
and good-byes
freeze to the lips
of the sun.
From now on
wars are
self-employed,
and time stirs
the pendulum of fear,
as though conducting
a Bach's concerto.
Nights inside a glass
with a glittering
tea-spoon

inspire,
like they used to,
the springtime uprising
of hope.

The Flood

The earth's salt heals
wounded hearts.
Silence behaving like
a tyrant;
distant groans; the pain
of poisoned
centuries...
The fog takes the sun away
for questioning;
the earthly hell
and the stars in a stir;
the cut veins
of doubt;
the horizon
scorched by anxiety...
The war rivers flow
into the ocean of death.
Noah floats high in the sky
followed by
a P.O.W. angel
wearing a white cloud,
enclosed in an envelope
—*poste restante*—
to be collected
in the future.

Time

Made
white-hot
by the pre-dawn
dew of insights,
looking surprised,
full of faults
of (mis)understanding,
generation after
generation,
here it comes,
time,
with its all-seeing eye.
Applauded by
the frantic evil,
the red rent,
the dues
of binding threads,
under the supervision
of belligerent fonts,
time sets sunrise fire
to the impregnable fortress
of events.

A Water-Melon Plantation

The monastic brotherhood
of water-melon seeds
in the forgotten red cells
of silence
amid the desert of solitude,
beyond the green casing
similar,
even identical
to a terrestrial globe,
with its mysterious furrows
of the roads
all bearing the same name,
leading to the spiritual realms
where souls
governed by heaven and the existential hell
create,
with naive angelic patience,
some other times
for Adam and Eve.

Trembita

The salt mines
of the European air,
the invisible hats
of Moldovan
and Hutsul villages...
Devastation
sets in here
caused by either drunkenness
or Goodness knows what else,
misleading people,
making them succumb
to rumours.
An epileptic wheel-cart
jogs along
the patches
of a poor district.
Apparently, they didn't
pay the rent in time
and didn't bow before somebody
who expected it of them.
And so, they're at a loss
this spring,
stuck between
thunder and lightning.
Congratulations,
here is a new,
a weird-looking
coat of paint
for your dilapidated
house.

Troy

Behind the pre-dawn
wall
of an unfulfilled love,
the capital city,
a picture from an earthly
memory,
some sacred, prancing
faces,
the foretaste of a choral
rain,
the quietude of organ
clouds...
A star beam
gets through the night mist
and pierces the heart.
Now tell me, Homer,
is it Helen's
shadow
that performs a wartime
ritual?
Is it that
wars,
like sea foam,
sleep on the deck
of epochs?

Rendezvous

Estranged nights,
boats with nowhere to dock,
faceless shadows
of leafless
idleness,
of algebraic
disturbances,
float in the aquarium
of the morning
with a heroic
smile,
as though
nothing has happened
to you, to me,
to my star
in winter or in spring,
neck-deep in the silence
of a sick mind.
For the pennies
of earthly happiness,
you want to sin
again and again.

The Plot

He was pathetic,
that soulless
killer
hiding
from his own
shadow.
He was crushed;
the black uproar
of the white lilac
surrounded him
in the capital city.
Spring kept its distance
from him;
it was suffering.
The raving dawn was
a red shroud.
The killer had
one more day
to live,
lengthy
as a thousand
years.

Happiness

On the outskirts of the
night of solitude,
bliss
builds a city
from winds' ashes
and rainwater.

The Sea

The sea
in the lotus position...
It throws
the stained glass windows
of the
red-terror-coloured
sunset
off the horizon's
pedestal.

The Air

The glass orbs of light
inside the winds' tomb;
the music of silence embraced
by the fearless eyes of the night;
the secret presence society;
the outline of an unfulfilled love,
and life under the heels of heavy clouds
in the era of asthmatic rains
at the seasons' crossing.

Souls

Stored
in the archives
of eternity,
the biographical
data
of human
souls.

Night

Breathless night;
deserts of doubt
between the moony oblivion
and the hell
of phenomena,
with their eyes unshut
and their fondness of
sunrise silence.

The World

The world deprived of
punctuation marks
runs barefoot
on the burning coals
of fading time,
and we scuttle along.
Don't ask us where
we're going;
no one will answer,
no one has a clue
what has happened to us,
or what lies ahead.
It is inertia,
the cynical life inertia
scurrying
in a squirrel wheel
of this planet
towards the ice age
of human
love.

Falling Stars

Bonfires burning...
each one
a flee market
of inspiration,
with mature stars,
—yours and mine—
in a free fall
of fortune.
Tell me who would venture
a random fall
from heaven,
from the invisible realm
onto the loyal Earth,
into the fogged sound
of love chimes
at the baroque hour of
captivating moments
that have deprived
the sky
of its gilding.
Rest your hands
the way pigeons
fold their wings;
wait for the flight
to end.

The Sense of Time

The sense of time,
the lapidary pain
of anonymous sins –
these are humanity's treasures
and subtle tears
of a tsunami
sliding down the cheek
on the lunar surface
of unfulfilled
dreams,
the ringing of crystal
seconds
resembling a flicker of words
behind the looking glass
   of silence.

Parallel Lines

The prima ballerina
has got lost in the brutal
ship cargo hold
packed with cigarettes.
There's pandemonium
and a stampede;
a smoking lady's hand
saves her
from oblivion
by accident,
by touch,
and the star lights up and fades
amid the smoke of the two
parallel lines
straightening up
on the lipstick deck.

September

In the fiercely transparent air of September
a Chopin morning sits down at the piano
and fingers lightly the white keys of the dawn.
Clouds wearing starched collars stroll slowly
along the embankment of the universe.
A fragile, inexplicable time.
A touch...

Hope

Until the sky invites me over, I will live
on this Earth. Hope has built a tiny cabin
in my heart; not even a cabin, more like a hut.
I keep my soul there. On bright mysterious nights,
angels flock together, naive like children.
In that cramped hut, they teach me
the penmanship of love.

Dreams

The postage stamps of dreams,
the flowering debt pits,
the interplay of dawn light
with naive
nightingale trills...
The follies of enamoured winds
swing the event hammock
along with foliage
and a lettuce salad
of time, of this spring
unfolding on the coast
of earthly visions
that entice me into the ocean
of your spellbound eyes.

Autumn

The city lifts yearning from the beggars; the roofs are plastered
with sweet jam. The birds will forget; the sky will be in mourning.
Fly away fast. The words "fare thee well" are shivering
on the platform; the house burns down like a candle stump;
moths have eaten the dawn; every dream is like a prison cell.
From our unsocial fates, we can only strike out
the start. Sadness blossoms on the windowsill
of autumn. This is a sign. Everything will settle.
Can you hear the footsteps? The astrologer cometh.
So the stars will emerge soon.

Snow

When a sun lily blossoms
amid swampy clouds
and the celestial bed is made up
and strewn with powdered sugar,
with the Turkish delight of premonitions,
a *divertissement* of disappointment
grows from the depth of summer
into autumn, and cold wise salt exudes,
in a foam-like way, through the pale-lit screen
as a hesitant dope. It all ends up in
cold turkey, in the shakes
of our communal century, the twenty-first...

Desert

A double-humped camel –
his Yes and No go away;
now we can hear a snake's
hiss: Why?

The Past

Only in your
pupils
can one see
the flame
of a bonfire
bitten to death
by the rain.

Spring Air

The resilient air
procrastinates
while feeble
rain chicks
fall
to the ground
from the nestling box
of the clouds.
The air
acquires resemblance
to a lined
notebook.
It's time to learn
miracle
penmanship.

Soundlessness

The transfiguration of soundlessness...
The joints of the wind ache with silence,
and multifaceted eyes
come to life inside the sand clock.
The day collapses, falls asleep,
and the riverbed of the shadows dries up
on the virgin palm of existence.
The detachment of a snowfall
on the lace-frame of time
embroiders diligently
the untruth
of bare hands
under the tiled roof
of feathery, fleecy,
flaky clouds.

Unspoken Words

In the front garden
of the ocean of silence,
atop a lifeless
maze
of shadows,
figurines
of unspoken
words
show themselves
momentarily.

Words

Chilled words
with wide cheekbones...
they resemble
a winter
that has returned to settle
in the vicinities of other people's palms.
They're destined to warm the snow,
fluffy, timid,
detached, disloyal
like love itself.

Chill

The heart feels
a winter chill;
it grows stronger
every day.
We're unable
to get warm
at the cold fires of poplars.

Silence

What is behind your silence?
My silence. And behind my silence
there is soundlessness, and behind soundlessness
there is eternity. So we've built a road from separation
to silence, from silence to soundlessness,
from soundlessness to eternity.

Word

A free, sensual, long-forgotten
text jotted down
in shorthand
in the original draft of time,
in the endless solitude of a white
winter-like clean sheet.
The beginning, the storm, the squall of passion...
No one knows from which expanses
the first word appears.

Rain

When it rains, a muffled life behind the fence
of love shows through the window-pane
like the black cherry of the night,
and clouds float across a snowy, sleepy dawn
towards the malachite garden
born in the warm ache of buzzing wasps.

Love

Love transpires through the rebellious green,
through the lost sun in the apogee of fate.
And the gifts of the red night, the riders of our
unfading eyes leave the universal bay that has positioned itself
by the sea – like a grateful horseshoe of Cimmerian happiness
in the backwoods of silence, your and mine.

Life

Since yesterday,
the dawn canvas
has been standing on an easel.
Don't believe that life
is a fantasy, an accident,
or a star sunk in the sky.
This is fine art for you; this is a cloud of delight,
an interchange of troubles and hopes.

A Disparate Life

While a timid rain is falling, contrive a disparate life. Don't believe that the long night river flows in the veins of silence. It's nothing but a dream, a hopeless flight of birds, a snake without a sting, without omissions and offenses, plain looking, like a written line staring into space from the lonely window of a stoolie.

After the Storm

On the second day after the storm
the weakened waves keep swaying
in synch with the dying wind, carrying to the shore
the indifferent approval of the horizon –
like a camel caravan in the desert.
Curious seagulls and barefoot children
stand on the porch of a desolate beach
begging for alms from the sea.
Towards the evening, the moonlight smoothens
the wrinkles on the muzzle of a sleeping beast
and treads a delicate path
leading beyond the horizon.

More poetry published by SurVision Books

Noelle Kocot. *Humanity*
(New Poetics: USA)
ISBN 978-1-9995903-0-7

Ciaran O'Driscoll. *The Speaking Trees*
(New Poetics: Ireland)
ISBN 978-1-9995903-1-4

Helen Ivory. *Maps of the Abandoned City*
(New Poetics: England)
ISBN 978-1-912963-04-1

Elin O'Hara Slavick. *Cameramouth*
(New Poetics: USA)
ISBN 978-1-9995903-4-5

John W. Sexton. *Inverted Night*
(New Poetics: Ireland)
ISBN 978-1-912963-05-8

George Kalamaras. *That Moment of Wept*
ISBN 978-1-9995903-7-6

Anton Yakovlev. *Chronos Dines Alone*
(Winner of James Tate Poetry Prize 2018)
ISBN 978-1-912963-01-0

Bob Lucky. *Conversation Starters in the Language No One Speaks*
(Winner of James Tate Poetry Prize 2018)
ISBN 978-1-912963-00-3

Christopher Prewitt. *Paradise Hammer*
(Winner of James Tate Poetry Prize 2018)
ISBN 978-1-9995903-9-0

Mikko Harvey & Jake Bauer. *Idaho Falls*
(Winner of James Tate Poetry Prize 2018)
ISBN 978-1-912963-02-7

Anatoly Kudryavitsky. *Stowaway*
(New Poetics: Ireland)
ISBN 978-1-9995903-2-1

Maria Grazia Calandrone. *Fossils*
Translated from Italian
(New Poetics: Italy)
ISBN 978-1-9995903-6-9

Sergey Biryukov. *Transformations*
Translated from Russian
(New Poetics: Russia)
ISBN 978-1-9995903-5-2

Anton G. Leitner. *Selected Poems 1981–2015*
Translated from German
ISBN 978-1-9995903-8-3

Our books are available to order via
http://survisionmagazine.com/books.htm

www.ingramcontent.com/pod-product-compliance
Lightning Source LLC
Chambersburg PA
CBHW061307040426
42444CB00010B/2557